THE VITALITY OF CHRISTIAN DOGMAS

THE VITALITY

OF

CHRISTIAN DOGMAS

AND THEIR POWER OF EVOLUTION

A Study in Religious Philosophy

BY

A. SABATIER, D.D.

DEAN OF THE FACULTY OF PROTESTANT THEOLOGY, PARIS

Translated by

MRS. EMMANUEL CHRISTEN

With a Preface by

THE VERY REVEREND THE HON. W. H. FREMANTLE, D.D.

DEAN OF RIPON

WIPF & STOCK · Eugene, Oregon

Wipf and Stock Publishers
199 W 8th Ave, Suite 3
Eugene, OR 97401

The Vitality of Christian Dogmas and Their Power of Evolution
A Study in Religious Philosophy
By Sabatier, A. and Christen, Emmanuel

Softcover ISBN-13: 979-8-3852-6500-8
Hardcover ISBN-13: 979-8-3852-6501-5
eBook ISBN-13: 979-8-3852-6502-2
Publication date 10/1/2025
Previously published by Adam & Charles Black, 1898

This edition is a scanned facsimile of the original edition published in 1898.

PREFACE

The accomplished lady who has translated the "short study" of Professor Sabatier has asked me to write a Preface to introduce it to those interested in theology in England; and I gladly respond to her wish, because the subject treated of is one which seems to be causing much anxious thought amongst us. It was touched upon in each of the three sermons at the opening of the Church Congress in October 1896. *The Archbishop of York spoke as follows:*[1]—

> *We cannot too earnestly contend for the faith once delivered to the saints, nor too rigorously regard as immutable the great foundations of Christian truth as they are contained in the Holy Scriptures and in*

1 *His text was* 1 *Thess.* v. 21 : *Prove all things; hold fast that which is good. Though the stress of the sermon was laid on matters of organisation and on the Roman controversy, the preacher did not hesitate to apply the principle of the text to the mode of statement of Christian truth.*

the Creeds of the Church. But the terms in which that truth has been stated, whether in the writings of individual Christians, however eminent, or in the Confessions of separate branches of the Church, may well require from time to time some reconsideration. . . . From age to age there ought to be a growing apprehension of the purport of the great message and of its bearing on personal needs, conditioned by the progress of knowledge and the special circumstances of each succeeding age. There is no reason why we should not reconsider our statements of doctrine . . . if under the guidance of the Holy Spirit they might be made more helpful to the welfare of the Church itself and to the comfort of individuals. . . . Are there not, in the estimation of most of us, one or two at least of the Thirty-nine Articles which might be brought more into accordance with the needs as well as the spirit of the present day?

The Bishop of Ballarat, the second of the Congress preachers, touched on another aspect of the matter.[1] *Truth, he con-*

[1] *The text was Deut.* xxix. 29: *The secret things belong unto the Lord our God: but those things which are revealed belong unto us and to our children for ever, that we may do all the words of this law.*

tended, should be clear, or, according to a word which he coined for the occasion, "epiphanious"; and the true faith is one which has a living grasp of these "epiphanious" truths, not a submission to that which is outside our apprehension. He said—

> *I am asked, Where, then, does faith come in, and the blessedness of those who have not seen and yet believe? I answer that true religious faith is precisely the faculty whereby we accept the "epiphanious" with the heart, and make surrender to it in our lives, and leave the mysterious in patient confidence with God. . . . The faith which yields a blind assent to mysterious dogmas because propounded by ecclesiastical authority is not the faith of Scripture at all; it is, in fact, fanaticism, and there is an unbelief which is preferable to it.*

Similarly, the third preacher, the Bishop of Rochester, urged the importance of humility in reference to our knowledge of divine things and in our statements about them.[1] *After speaking of the danger of over-definition, he continues—*

I infer that the truest and best type of Christian doctrine or teaching is that which is true to these conditions, which not only recognises them but abides in the consciousness of them, which realises a duty of ignorance as well as a duty of knowledge, which knows that Gnosticism is an abiding danger as well as Agnosticism, and that Christian theology must find place for the truth that is in both, and must be wisely silent as well as bravely speak. . . . How boldly have great dogmatists, looking back, acknowledged that dogma is a necessary evil, laying stress on both words.

These utterances seem to show a consciousness that it is a great need of our day to make Christian truth real and living, and that this involves at times some alteration in its expression; and the remarkable concurrence of the three ser-

[1] *The text was Ps.* cxxxi. 1: *Lord, my heart is not haughty, nor mine eyes lofty: neither do I exercise myself in great matters, or in things too high for me.*

mons in this may be taken to show that the need is felt very widely, and does not belong to any special school. It appears to me that, in this state of the Christian mind, Professor Sabatier's work may be of great use. It will be seen at once that he gives no support to the indiscriminate denunciations of dogma which are sometimes heard. He looks upon it, on the contrary, as necessary to the very existence of Christianity. But he shares to the full the desire that it should be not the dead form of past convictions but the living expression of Christian piety.

The changes which this necessity from time to time involves he describes as having three forms. Some dogmas simply pass away because they represented ideas which have ceased to exist. Some remain, but by a process which he terms "Intussusception" are modified or intensified in their meaning. And in some cases new ideas come into prominence and need an expression either by the revival of old formulas or by the creation of new. Of these processes that which he terms "Intussusception" seems to be by far the most fruitful, especially as regards that which will be felt on all hands to be the most delicate matter, the expression given to the Christian faith in the Creeds. He fully admits the extent to which Greek philosophy and Roman law entered into some of these expressions, and consequently that their outward form belongs to a circle of ideas somewhat different from our own. "We can no more think in Greek than we can speak Greek." But, while claiming freedom from too close an addiction to the outward form he appears to have no wish to change it: his effort is to throw into it the full moral force of the truth which it was intended to express. If I understand him rightly, he would wish such expressions as those of the Nicene Creed which assert our Lord's divine nature to be maintained, but to be felt to assert more than their metaphysical character would mean to men of our day. He would show their moral bearing and get us to use them as implying our Lord's supremacy, as one with a God who is essentially a God of righteousness and of love, over our consciences and over the whole range of the moral world. This would certainly be the application made by theologians of the Church of England, as it would be my own, of the principles of criticism for which he contends.

The work is in the form of an introductory lecture, and it would not be fair to the author to limit him to the special illustrations which he gives, with some of which we may not wholly agree. But I think it will be felt to be full of suggestion, and will help men to think out for themselves the problems with which it deals.

Though it touches on many matters which have been the theme of controversy, it is written in no controversial spirit; and I hope it may be read in England not as intended to uphold any one-sided view of theology, but as a sincere contribution to the solution of a problem which is felt to be one of pressing interest.

W. H. FREMANTLE.

THE DEANERY, RIPON,
January 1898.

THE
VITALITY OF CHRISTIAN DOGMAS
AND THEIR
POWER OF EVOLUTION

At the risk of running counter to some accepted opinions concerning dogmas, we purpose here to study their life and their power of evolution. No other subject is beset by more prejudices, and in no other is the mind more easily satisfied with superficial ideas. One prejudice, for instance, is that which makes so many people say that dogmas are dead or dying. Before 1830 Jouffroy wrote his celebrated philosophical essay called *How Dogmas*

End. Sixty years have elapsed since then, and another philosopher of the same school, M. Caro, has found it opportune to write another essay called *How Dogmas Revive.* In truth, dogmas do not die, they become transformed.

It is a curious fact that the very people who prophesy the death of dogmas are those who believe them to be immutable; and thus they make a second assumption to justify the first. Everything around us changes: our knowledge, our philosophy, our customs, our mental state even,—all are modified in the course of centuries. How, then, can it be possible that metaphysical formulas, which constitute dogmas, should impose themselves on our thought for ever? On what ground, we venture on our side to ask, can men rest the notion that dogmas are necessarily stationary? Are they not, as history presents them to us, in a perpetual course of transformation? If they have altered in the past, what is to prevent them from being modified in the future? The fact is this. A Church which is deluding itself with the false assumption of infallibility has said of its own dogmas, what a General of the Company of Jesus is alleged to have said on one occasion of the Jesuits: *Sint ut sunt, aut non sint.*[1] And this affirmation, which is nothing less than a defiance thrown in the face of history, has forced itself so thoroughly on Papists, on philosophers, and even on Protestants, at least in France, that we evangelical theologians, who are made free from this bondage by the Spirit of Christ,

[1] Let them be as they are, or let them not be at all.

run the risk of shocking them all, or at least of surprising them considerably, by trying to show that this imaginary immutability of dogmas is a fiction, and that they have, in reality, like everything else, their inevitable and natural evolution.

But here, again, we are confronted by a third assumption, which is closely connected with the two former. We allude to the confusion which is continually made between dogmas and religion. Men come to believe that dogmas constitute the very essence of religion, and from that moment, whether they are believers or unbelievers, they equally imagine, in all good conscience, that to criticise the one is to destroy the other. This error arises from the strange idea still prevailing among us, though it is refuted a hundred times over by a careful psychology, that religion is essentially a metaphysical theory, a branch of erudition. It is said that dogmas produce religion, and that, when the cause is taken away, the effect must disappear; and men forget, what religious history teaches most clearly, that it is religion, on the contrary, which produces dogmas, and that it produces them naturally, as a tree produces flowers and fruit. In life, the awakening of feeling always precedes that of thought. And so religion exists as emotion, or sentiment, or vital instinct, before it is transformed either into intellectual notions or into rites. This primary and inner emotion is so truly the life of religion, that where it no longer exists, be it in the most correct dogmas or the most magnificent worship, there is no longer any true religion.

It is good, no doubt, and even necessary, that religious feeling should, at a certain stage, take stock of its own ideas and express itself in notions; but these notions should no more be mistaken for religion than thought should be mistaken for language. They may, and do, vary, without religion suffering any real loss from this in its expansive force. The criticism of dogma most commonly contributes to its development in the same way that pruning a tree hastens the progress and doubles the power of its vitality. If this point could once be made thoroughly clear, it would, I think, in all probability lighten up many others. If we could succeed in presenting dogmas—not as absolute and immutable formulas, but in their power of evolution—as being the result of the sustained and progressive effort of the religious consciousness, we should, perhaps, make them more acceptable to philosophers. If we could only make believers understand this essential independence of Christian piety, and consider this historical evolution of dogmas—the very mention of which frightens them to-day—as an advantage and a safeguard, we should, perhaps, also win back their confidence, and remove many of the stumbling-blocks which lie in the path of theology.

Such is, in my intention, the object of this essay. My reflections will be directed to three points: First, I propose to show that dogmas are not dead things; that they have an inner life, and develop continually by a kind of secret and irresistible growth. Secondly, I shall explain how this evolution of dogmas which this living power makes possible, is rendered absolutely necessary by the laws of history. Finally, we must endeavour to find out what part modern dogmatics can and ought to take in this work of continual transformation. We cannot conceive any better way than this of giving an insight into the true nature and the absorbing interest of the study of dogmatics.

I

It is a truth which has become almost a commonplace in linguistics, that languages are organisms and that words have a life of their own, quite analogous to that of animals or of plants. It is through this vital power which belongs to them that their continuance and their transformations are explained. Each dialect, so long as it is spoken, is in motion, and it may be said that the intensity of its life is identical with this power of evolution. It is the same with the dogmas of a Church, which form likewise a living organism, and which are, if rightly considered, only a kind of theological language by which the consciousness of the Church or the piety of its members reveals itself outwardly, and grows stronger by this self-revelation. The more one thinks of this, the more one must be struck with the justness of this analogy and the light which it sheds on the very basis of our subject. What words and sentences are to thought, dogmatic formulas are to the religious experience of the conscience. We are now in a position to make a general affirmation, which is this: Just as the life of a language does not lie in the sonorousness of words or in the correctness of phrases, but only in the secret energy of the thought and in the genius of the people who speak it, so the principle of the life of dogmas must not be sought in the logic of ideas or in more or less exact theoretic formulas, but only in the religious life itself, that is to say, in the practical piety of the Church which professes them. Dogma, in a word, is the language of faith.

In order to feel this warm and intense life of dogmas, and to see how supple and malleable it makes them, one must not seek them in the Confessions of Faith or symbolical books in which they are registered and classed in order. One must no more be satisfied with studying them in those catalogues than one must take the words of a modern language as they lie in the dictionary. Words and dogmas there appear, and are, dead and motionless, for they lie there in a kind of tomb. But to feel the life of words, to see the process by which they are modified, and take infinite shades of colour, and burgeon and put out innumerable suckers, you must take them from the lips of your fellow-men in daily intercourse. It is only at this furthest point, where it blends with life, that one can realise that a living language is eminently capable of fusion, and that it is like a bar of iron which has been made red hot in the fire, and which the smith with his hammer and anvil can forge into the most various shapes.

Dogmas offer the same phenomenon. It is only in the compilations which go by the name of books of Symbolics, that we find them in their state of fixity, in a form of irreproachable and frozen orthodoxy. But watch them in the daily practice of individual or public piety; listen to the prayers which rise from hearts moved by feeling; note what each believer finds in them or adds on his own account to these venerable and customary expressions of religion; catch them in their flight, so to say, in popular sermons, in the teaching of the young, in daily practical applications, and you will be quite surprised to find these apparently hieratical formulas so easy, so undulating, so rich in meaning and in shade, and susceptible of so many interpretations. When we use a word of common language we necessarily bathe it, so to say, in the living experience of our soul, and it comes out of that bath all coloured by our inner emotions. In the same way, when we use a dogmatic formula in the spirit of piety, we bathe it in the religious emotion of our heart, and it necessarily gains from this some essential modification. No one but a parrot will repeat constantly the same words in the same way, and none but irreligious and indifferent minds will repeat the old dogmas without some addition or subtraction.

These practical and everyday interpretations of consecrated formulas differ in the same proportion as believers who employ them differ in their degree of culture. I see a large assembly gathered in one of our churches for worship. In this assembly some are poor old women, very ignorant and somewhat superstitious; some are men of the middle class, possessing some tincture of literature; some are wise men and philosophers who have meditated on Kant and Hegel, and even professors of theology who are penetrated to the marrow with the spirit of criticism. All of these bow down their hearts and worship; all speak the same tongue learned in childhood; all repeat with heart and lip: *I believe in God the Father Almighty.* Is there on earth a sight more touching or anything nearer to heaven? All these minds who are so different from each other, and who would perhaps be incapable of understanding each other in the sphere of the intellect alone, are yet in real communion with each other; they are penetrated and animated by the same religious sentiment. The moral unity spoken of by Jesus when He said,

That they may be one, even as we are one, is for the moment realised on earth. But do you suppose that the word *God*, when it is pronounced by all those lips, summons up the same image to each one of those minds? To the old woman who remembers the illuminations of her large Bible, the Father Eternal appears with a long white beard and brilliant eyes shining like coals of fire. Her neighbour would smile at the simplicity of this anthropomorphism. He has in his mind the theistic idea as it was rationally set forth to him in the course of lectures of philosophy he attended at College. But again this idea will seem coarse to the disciple of Kant, who knows that all positive idea of God is contradictory, and who, in order to escape contradiction, takes refuge in the *unknowable.* And yet, for all of them, the dogma of God subsists, and it is because it is still living that it lends itself to so many different interpretations; but observe that it is living only because it serves as the expression of a piety felt by all these believers and common to them all.

Let us now go a step further, and analyse dogma in order to separate clearly the elements of which it is composed. These elements are two in number: first, at the root, a mystical and practical element, the religious element proper, which flows from the experience or from the piety of a Church; this is the living and fruitful principle of dogma; secondly, an intellectual or theoretical element, a judgment of the mind, a philosophical proposition, which serves at once to envelop and to express the first.

Now, the relation which unites and amalgamates these two elements in dogma is no arbitrary thing; it is an organic and necessary relation. Let us go back to the origin of the *processus* of religion, to the formation of the first and simplest doctrinal formulas. We find man, when brought face to face with some one of the great spectacles of nature, feeling his own weakness and his dependence in the presence of the mysterious power which is there revealed, and trembling with fear and with hope. This tremor is the primary religious emotion. But to the mind this emotion necessarily implies a certain relation between the subject which is conscious of it and the object which caused it. Then, when once the man's thought is awakened, he will necessarily translate this relation into an intellectual statement. Thus, for instance, to express this relation the believer will cry out, "God is great!" marking, in so doing, the infinite disproportion which exists between his own being and the universal Being who causes him to tremble. He obeys the same necessity which, in the ordinary process, makes him express his thought by means of language. The religious emotion, which is a feeling, thus transforms itself in the mind into a notion of our relation to the object; that is to say, into an intellectual notion which becomes its equivalent image or representation of our feeling. But intellectual notion and religious emotion remain essentially different in their nature. The intellectual notion may, in expressing itself, and with the aid of the imagination, help to renew or to strengthen emotion; dogma may awaken piety; but these two must not be confounded. The notion is, as it were, an algebraic expression which represents ideally a given dimension without being the dimension itself. This is a thing which must be well understood if we are to prevent disastrous confusion. In the case of religion and dogma, the intellectual element is only the symbolical expression of religious experience.

An observation suggested by the history of dogmas fully confirms this relative and subordinate character of the intellectual element in relation to the mystical. It is a remarkable fact that the promulgation of each dogma has been imposed upon the Church by some practical necessity. Each time the Church has set itself to work to make laws in matters of dogma, the object has always been to put an end to some theological controversy which threatened to create a schism, or to reply to attacks or accusations which, if they had been allowed to gain credit, would have been dangerous. It has never taken to that extreme measure except when defending its very life. Nothing is more false than to represent the Fathers of the Councils or the members of the synods as theorists, or even as theologians by profession, gathered together solely by the impulse of speculative zeal to resolve metaphysical enigmas. They were men of action and not of speculation; they were valiant priests and pastors who understood their mission as soldiers in full battle, and whose main care was to save the Church, its life, its unity, its honour, for which they were ready to die as soldiers die for their country. But this being so, is it not evident that the dogmas thus elaborated and made into laws were rigidly determined by contemporary controversies and difficulties; at least, that for the terms in which they were drawn up, and for the form of thought, these dogmas depended on the circumstances which gave them birth; and that, when the controversies or the circumstances have altered, it has been found necessary, and must always be so, to modify the old formulas, or to discover new ones? This is indeed so true, that the formulas which, for instance, caused the heresy of Arius to be condemned, became themselves heretical when, later, it was necessary to fight against the heresy of the Monophysites, and when, later still, Catholic orthodoxy was compelled to formulate solutions entirely contradictory of those made before. What can be more unreasonable than to elevate to the dignity of eternal axioms dogmas which have the character of historical contingency so plainly written on their foreheads?

The intellectual element, then, in dogmas will always remain the element which is essentially changeable. It is the matter united to the germ, and which is being continually transformed by the movement of the life. The reason of this is plain. We were saying just now that a religious emotion, like every other sensation, is commuted into a notion which fixes the relation—a relation implied by the emotion itself—between the subject and the object. But what is this notion to be? With what materials, with what concepts, will the religious man build it up? With those, evidently, which are within his reach. This means that his religious formula will always depend upon his state of intellectual culture. As a child, he will think and speak of religion as a child. The reason and the language of religion have gone through the same stages as reason in general. In religion, as in everything else, men have begun with poetry and picture before reasoning or discussing in prose. Later on, when the Fathers of the Church had learned the philosophy of Plato, of Aristotle, or of the Stoics, we shall find them constructing their dogmas as philosophers; that is to say, they thought and spoke as such.

Many Christians imagine that God has revealed dogmas to us in the Bible; and they will accuse us, in speaking as we do, of denying revelation. God forbid! We believe with all our soul in divine revelation, and in its particular action in the soul of the prophets, of the apostles—most of all in that of Christ. The question is only whether divine revelation consisted in doctrines and in dogmatic formulas. We say no. God has created nothing useless, and since these doctrines and these formulas could be, and were in fact, conceived by man's intellect, He left to man the care of elaborating them. But God, in entering into contact with the soul, has made it go through a certain religious experience, out of which, by means of reflection, dogmas have issued. Thus, what constitutes revelation, what should be the *norm* of our life, is the creative and fruitful religious experience as it originally existed in the soul of the prophets, of Christ, and of the apostles. We need have no anxiety. So long as this redeeming and renovating experience continues and renews itself in Christian souls, Christian dogmas may, indeed, be modified; they are in no danger of dying.

Here, the question may be put to us: "Why should dogmas be preserved? Why should we consent any longer to this imperfect amalgam of pure religious life and philosophical notions which are in their nature transitory? Why cannot we take religion in its naked state?" Thus spoke, only a short time since, a theological school, a kind of Christian positivism, which asked for a religion without dogmas, and consequently without worship. But have you observed what happens when these views are followed out? When you suppress Christian dogma, Christianity itself is suppressed; when you put aside absolutely all religious doctrine, religion itself is destroyed. How many great and eternal things there are in the universe which for us never exist in a pure and isolated condition! This is the case with all the forces of nature. Thought, in order to exist, must incarnate itself in language. Words cannot be identified with thought, yet they are necessary to it. The hero of fiction who said he could only think when he spoke, was not so ridiculous as he was considered, for this hero is everybody. In the same way, the soul reveals itself to us only by the body to which it is joined. Who has ever seen life outside of living matter? Who can grasp and separate in the acorn the fruitful germ from the *fecula*[1] with which it is amalgamated? It is the same with religious life in its relation to the doctrines and to the rites through which it is manifested. A religious life which did not express itself would be unconscious, and would be incapable of communicating itself. It is therefore quite irrational to speak of a religion without dogma and without worship. Orthodoxy proves itself right a hundred times over as against rationalism or mysticism, when it proclaims that it is necessary for a church to formulate its faith in doctrines without which the objects

[1] The pulpy substance of the seed.

of the religious consciousness would remain confused and unrecognisable.

If, then, it is a necessity that life should become incarnate in an organism—thought in language, and religion in dogma—it is just as inevitable, on the other hand, that language should be modified, and that dogmas should be transformed. This law of life suffers no exception in nature. Consequently, we shall look on it as an error or an illusion into which orthodoxy in its turn falls, when it denies or tries to stop the incessant metamorphosis. It is precisely by its movement, and by perpetually exchanging for fresh material the elements which constitute it, that an organism reveals itself. When languages are no longer renewed, they become dead. So also, if dogmas remain motionless, they become deprived of life. They are like some old coat of armour which hangs on the walls of a museum; it outlines the figure of some warrior of old times; but strike it, and you find that it is empty and sounds hollow.

We see, then, that dogmas have in them a power of evolution. We must now ask how this evolution proceeds. The analogies we have pointed out between the life of dogmas and that of languages are still true to the end. Now, a language is modified in three ways: (1) by desuetude, that is, by the disappearance of certain words, the meaning of which has vanished; (2) by "inward reception,"[1] or the faculty which words possess of acquiring new meanings, without changing their outward form;

[1] The author uses the Latin word *Intus-susceptio.*

(3) by the revival of old words, or the creation of new, *i.e.* by what we call neologism.

The history of dogmas shows clearly enough these three kinds of variations. Some religious formulas die out by desuetude. The idea they used to express has vanished from our consciousness; they are no longer in use, and will be sooner or later quite forgotten. Need we cite examples of this? The history of dogmas is strewn with such forms, which for us are empty, and like bleached and faded shells, deserted by their living inhabitants. You know what a vast place was occupied in the mind of the early Church by demons and the idea of demoniacal possession; men's minds were haunted by it. There was even among the clergy a class of priests whose business was to drive them out. There still exist prayers and formulas of exorcism used frequently in those times, as may be seen in the writings of Tertullian. All that has disappeared, at least for our Protestant consciousness. In the same way, the belief in the Devil, that is to say, in the personal, historical Devil, acting supernaturally in our life, is seen to be moribund. He no longer appears to people, either by night or by day. Luther, when he threw his inkstand at his head, inflicted on him a wound of which he is dying. The ink had more effect than the holy water to exorcise him for ever.

The second mode of evolution, or "inward reception," works with a still more sovereign energy. We have kept, and still repeat, the dogmas of early times; but we pour into them unconsciously a new meaning. The terms do not change, but the ideas and their interpretation are renewed with each generation. This is particularly the work of the theologian. We spend our life, consciously or unconsciously, in putting new wine into old bottles. There is not a single dogma dating from two or three centuries back which is repeated with the same meaning as in its origination. We still speak of the inspiration of the prophets and of the apostles, of atonement, of the Trinity, of the divinity of Christ, of miracles; but, whether in a greater or less degree, we understand them differently from our fathers. The river flows on, even when the waters are apparently stagnant at the surface.

But the elasticity of words and formulas has a limit. There comes a time when the new wine causes the old bottles to break, and when it becomes necessary for the Church to make new vessels to receive it. Then new words appear in languages and new dogmas in theology. It is thus that the dogmas of justification by faith and of universal priesthood came into prominence in the sixteenth century. New dogmas, do we call them? Rather, we should say, old ones rising again with new energy. Here also the verses of Horace remain ever true. It would seem as if we had been simply making a comment upon them.

> "Ut silvæ foliis pronos mutantur in annos,
> . . . . . .
> Multa renascentur quæ jam cecidere, cadentque
> Quæ nunc sunt in honore vocabula."

> "As leaves in woods are changed with changing years,
> So words that once have fall'n may live again;
> While many now in honour'd use may fall."

II

These principles having now been firmly established, let us endeavour to apply them to the history of dogmatic Christianity in order to test their value. We have come to understand how the evolution of dogmas is possible; we must now see why it is necessary.

Jesus, the Great Sower, often compared His word to a grain of wheat. No image could be deeper or more accurate. His words have indeed been a living seed, and bear fruit for ever. Now, in a grain of wheat there is a germ, a mysterious power, that we cannot grasp; it is the power of the life which comes from God. In the same way, the words of Christ contain a *nescio quid divinum*,[1] a germ which has come out of His consciousness as Saviour of mankind and Son of God, and which communicates a creative virtue to all His acts and words. But in the grain of wheat there is, as well as the new germ which no scalpel can seize and separate, a certain substance, a *fecula*, necessary to the germ in order that it may manifest itself and produce its effects. Now, this external matter can be analysed; it is compounded of nitrogen, glucose, albumen, lime, etc. Similarly, in the words of Christ, the living germ, the creative power of the gospel, is found amalgamated with a certain Hebraic *fecula*, from the very fact that Christ was a Hebrew, heir to His race, and that He spoke a Semitic dialect. And it

[1] Something undefinable, but divine.

is for this reason that, in spite of its undeniable originality, the gospel appears to us in its first Palestinian form as a Hebraic phenomenon; and such, indeed, it is, in the language and the circle of general customs and hereditary conceptions in which it is enclosed: such as its notion of justice, its metaphysical notion of God, its Messianic ideas, its apocalyptical hopes, etc. We can scarcely imagine Christ being born anywhere but in Judæa, or at another time than at the close of the history of Israel. All plants do not grow alike, and are not equally fruitful in every climate; there is a linking and co-ordination in God's plan. But if we make an effort of thought, and suppose for an instant that Christ belonged to a different race, came into a different kind of civilisation, and spoke a different language; that he appeared, for instance, in China, or in the India of Manu or of Buddha, is it not evident that the original form of the gospel would have been quite different? and does not this very hypothesis show the historical and contingent character of the form which it took in Israel?

Only, what we can and ought to state is, that this *fecula* of Hebraism is, in the primitive gospel, reduced to the minimum; in the authentic discourses of Jesus, the creative and revealing principle is connected with the most elementary, and consequently the most lasting ideas. It has often been said that the Hebrew race was, from a philosophical point of view, the poorest of all the civilised races; it has existed for centuries on two or three conceptions. No doubt it is for that reason that God chose it in preference to another, and sowed in it the germ of the powerful religious creation which has sprung from it, so that the principle of the gospel, being as free as possible from human formulas, should better appear in its naked power. It is none the less true that the plant which issued from a divine seed in Hebraic soil, took, and was bound to take for the time being, a Hebraic appearance. What we are here noticing is the law of adaptation to the environment, which will find many another application.

A few years later, St. Paul comes upon the scene. He sows the Christian seed in profusion in the vast field of Hellenic civilisation, which, by long lying fallow, had doubled its productive capacity. You know well what deep deposits of soil had gone to the composition of that rich vegetable mould. Upon it the deposits of ancient Greek poetry, of the philosophy of Socrates, of the science of Aristotle, of the ethics of Stoicism, and of the wisdom of Alexandria, had successively settled down. The pure and graceful, though somewhat fragile and meagre plant which flourished on the rocky and dry hills of Judæa here takes all at once such unexpected proportions and such a new appearance, that after three centuries it is scarcely recognisable. It has become, in the matter of organisation, worship, and dogmas, a large tree with powerful branches and thick foliage. Then appear, one by one, the luxuriant vegetation of the Gnostic systems, the green and vigorous leafage of the learned theology of Clement and Origen, the theory of the *Logos*, derived in a direct line from Philo, the first of the Fathers of the Church, from which issued, in due time, the dogmas of Nice and of Chalcedon. What a distance there is between the dogmatic Christianity of the fourth and fifth centuries and the Messianic gospel preached by the Master on the shores of the Lake of Galilee! Here the rare and pure moral ideas of Hebraism; there, all the fundamental notions of Greek logic and metaphysics.

How can we indeed explain the astonishing formation of the great Catholic dogmas of that time, otherwise than by the mingling of the principle of the gospel with the alloy of Hellenic thought? Let us examine more closely the construction of this dogmatic Christianity. With what materials was the edifice built? From what quarry came the facing stones employed in it? What architect designed the plan? With what style can we most suitably connect it? The Roman Church declares that it all comes from the Bible. This is a great illusion. Origen and Augustine, the theologians of the time, no doubt did find it all in the Bible, but it was by means of the allegorical interpretation, the same by which Philo found it possible to read the Platonic and Stoic philosophy into the books of Moses. Unfortunately this marvellous kind of alchemy which made possible and even easy the transmutation of all the various modes of expression into each other, has, for the thought of our time, lost all authority and all power. The expedients which it supplied for dogmatics can no longer be of any use to us. The philosophical substructure of the Catholic dogmas has remained as thoroughly Greek as was the language in which they were first of all drawn up.

Such, then, being the case, by what right can we proclaim eternal and immutable a system of dogmatics, the origin and particular character of which is revealed so clearly by history? This system suited the Greco-Roman world, no doubt, and it is also, doubtless, to this very suitability that it owes its triumph. Is not this just a reason why it can no longer suit our own, unless it be admitted that our civilisation and our philosophy have no right to differ from the civilisation and the philosophy of the last centuries of the Roman Empire? Do you not see what the Church has done by proclaiming the infallibility of the ancient dogmas? It has not only decreed the immutability of the gospel; it has decreed the infallibility of Aristotle's logic and of Plato's philosophy. It was quite natural in the Middle Ages that Aristotle should be deified and placed on a level with the prophets and the apostles. Let Roman Catholicism, if it will, remain faithful to this tradition; we will not dispute with it; but that Protestantism, whose principle has been to break this very tradition and to come back from human opinions to the Word of God, should be subjected to this tradition is a thing which we can only recognise as a posthumous revenge, in the bosom of the Protestant Churches themselves, of the Roman principle from which they thought that they had escaped for ever.

We do not mean to say that everything in the old formulas is to be condemned; they contain, on the contrary, many great and excellent ideas which still retain their truth and their power; we merely say that they are not absolute, and cannot be forced upon the Christian mind by authority. It is always with notions borrowed from the philosophy of its environment and the science of the day that the Christian spirit builds up its dogmas. But, since this philosophy and this science are constantly developing, they carry dogma along with them in their evolution. All those who have any real feeling for history, feel also that everything is liable to change, even our way of thinking. Have you considered why it is that certain things, as they were imaged in men's minds in the past, seem to us absurd or grotesque? It is because we have lost the faculty of understanding them. It is as impossible for us to think in Greek as to talk in Greek. Since the Middle Ages, two or three intellectual revolutions have taken place, which have separated us profoundly from antiquity, and have completely changed both the outer and the inner world in which we live. It will suffice to recall them in a few words to show the decay of Greco-Roman dogmatic Christianity and the necessity imposed upon us of renewing it, provided that Christianity is yet strong enough to hear and to respond to the call of God.

The first of these revolutions is a religious revolution: the Reformation of the sixteenth century. The formation of our specific consciousness as Protestant Christians dates from that time. Now, what was the evangelical reformation but the breaking away from the tradition of the Church, the foundation and solid framework of which were the dogmatics of the great Councils? In breaking the yoke of Church authority, did not the reformers break also the very basis on which these old dogmas had been built? In appealing to the pure word of God against the doctrines of tradition, what did our fathers do but, at the very least, mark as questionable these very dogmatics of the great Councils? After having protested against the infiltration of pagan customs and superstitions, either in the code of morals of the Church, or in her organisation and hierarchy, or in her worship and rites, how and why should the ancient philosophy which entered into the construction of her dogmas be declared too sacred to be touched?

On the other hand, the Reformation did something far greater: it renewed the very essence of the Christian conscience by its fundamental doctrine of justification by faith alone. Until then, man was saved by adhesion to the symbols of the Catholic Church and by obedience to its commandments. Justification by faith (and faith here means the confidence of the heart in the Gospel of God) frees the Christian from the tutelage of priesthood and from the slavery to symbols. Maintaining that man cannot be saved unless he believes such and such a theological doctrine, comes to the same as saying that he cannot be saved unless he does such and such a deed; it is adding to or putting in the place of faith some other condition of salvation. This second principle of the Reformation, therefore, explodes the ancient fabric of formulas still more conspicuously by substituting in matters of dogma the inner principle of Christian experience for the outer principle of Church authority; it turns Christianity into a moral life instead of a system of metaphysics. Is it not right and necessary, therefore, to give to the new principle of the Reformation, in the sphere of dogma, a new and adequate theological expression?

The religious revolution of the sixteenth century thus altered the pivot of the Christian conscience. At the same epoch there was commencing a scientific revolution which was destined to alter the pivot of the outer world. I refer to that connected with the names of Copernicus and Kepler, and later on with those of Galileo, Newton, and Laplace. Modern astronomy and geology have completely changed the framework and the horizon of our philosophy. We have all had, like Pascal, a vision of the infinity of space and time which has astounded us. How different is our cosmos from that of our forefathers! That was limited on every side. The earth, flat and round, surrounded by the river Ocean, formed the centre; above, the sky was a crystal vault revolving with the stars. Above that again, other skies and spheres up to the number of seven. These formed a kind of seven-storied edifice, at the top of which the supreme God, resting from His great work of Creation, sat commanding and superintending the whole of His small universe. Below the earth were other stages underground, the infernal regions, the low and dark places where the devils and the wicked were banished and tormented. Such was the popular cosmography of those days, as it had been suggested to the scarcely developed mind of man by the appearance of things and by the first observations of his senses.

Now, we must neither forget nor ignore the fact that this primitive cosmography has come into the composition and drawing up of many dogmatic or religious formulas, which, for this very reason, are now decrepit and antiquated. In reading not only the writings of the Fathers, but also the Old and the New Testament, we meet, at each step, with certain statements which exegesis must put aside or interpret in a different sense from that which the authors had in mind. When St. Paul, for instance, says in his Epistle to the Philippians (ii. 10), in speaking of Christ, that the *ἐπουρανίοι*, or inhabitants of the superior spheres, the *ἐπιγείοι*, or inhabitants of the earth, and the *καταχθονίοι*, or beings of the lower regions, must bow the knee before Christ, it is evident that he has in mind cosmographical regions which for us exist no more. The religious thought expressed by St. Paul, namely, that the value of the person of Christ in relation to the whole universe is infinite, remains true for our conscience; but the form in which he expressed it is dead.

Another time, St. Paul declares that he was caught up to the third heaven.[1] Where

[1] 2 Cor. xii. 2.

are we to look for this third heaven to-day? For there is no longer any going up or coming down in infinite space. For the orthodox, just as much as for the unorthodox, these words of St. Paul are only a metaphor to express a particular psychological state which we call ecstasy. But if this be so with regard to the ascension of Paul, what are we to think of that of Christ? Are we to picture it to ourselves as a real, material asçension in the outer space? If He went up in that way, where did He stop? Where was it possible for Him to meet with God, even if He had passed through all physical space up to infinity? Here, again, although affirming the spiritual and moral glorification of Christ in God, I doubt whether any enlightened Christian can represent to himself the ascension of Christ exactly in the same way as Luke did, when he wrote the first chapter of the Acts of the Apostles.

How can we avoid saying the same as to the descent of Christ into hell? We cannot conceive it in the same way as did the early Christians, because our world is no longer what their world was. When the Church, then, repeats the words, "He ascended into heaven," "He descended into hell," with the ancient creed of the first centuries, it no doubt confesses precious religious and moral truths which must be maintained; but it conceives them as entirely separate from the childish cosmography with which primitive Christian thought had combined them. They are nothing but survivals of expression, ways of speaking, or metaphors, exactly like those we still use, without, however, being deceived by them, when we say, "The sun is setting," or, "The sun is rising."

This cosmography of early times is equally inherent to the dogma of Christ's *parousia*[1] on earth, and to the whole *scenario* of the Messianic eschatology, as it is found, for example, in the last discourses of Jesus and in the Apocalypse. These, again, are images which we can no longer accept otherwise than as symbols. It is impossible for us to realise Hell and Paradise geographically, and to conceive the dogma of eternal punishment exactly as did the Christians of early times. On all these points, the decisive changes of conception which we are noting have come about of themselves; there are others

[1] The Greek word for "presence," sometimes translated "coming." See 2 Thess. ii. 1, and margin.

where resistance has been stronger, but where dogmatic evolution is none the less necessary.

As a last example, let us take the creation. Our knowledge of the universe having been modified as we have just stated, it is nothing more than natural that the old formulas of the creation should no longer suffice to explain its origin and continual development. Let me quote some words recently spoken by one of our colleagues at Montauban, Mr. Leenhardt, which have a special authority on this subject, because he is both a theologian and a man of science: "If there is one indisputable result of all the geological studies pursued up to this day, it is, that nature did not come out of the hand of the Creator, as Minerva came out of the brain of Jupiter.

As we see it and admire it now, it is the conclusion of a long work of transformation." And he continued: "This result has a philosophical bearing which cannot be exaggerated. It leads to nothing short of a profound modification of the idea theologians have formed of the creative action of God."

The traditional dogma of creation is indeed bursting asunder on two points. In the face of the slow and constant evolution of the universe from the gaseous nebula up to the life of our planet and the organic and moral life which is developed upon it, it is impossible to reduce the creation into one creative act alone, after which God took His rest. There is no Sabbath for the eternal *Workman*. "He worketh until now," according to the word of Jesus,[1] and

[1] John v. 17.

the theologians of our Reformation were right in identifying the creation with Providence. God is creating incessantly in time and space; that is what we now perceive in the history of nature.

But this is not all: this fact, once admitted, leads to another of greater consequence still. In introducing the idea of succession in divine creation, we necessarily introduce into it, at the same time, the idea of relativity; that is, that the first divine creation, being taken as a starting-point, was not and could not be absolute and perfect.

The old dogma starts with the axiom that God, being Himself perfection, can only create a perfectly finished world at a single stroke. This is the gnostic idea on which the whole system of emanation by descending progression is founded. In admitting this metaphysical axiom, and rejecting the systems of successive emanation, the Church, in order to explain the presence of sin, of pain, and of death in the world, was compelled to derive them from the moral fall of Adam. And this is what has been done. But, in the present day, when we have before us fossils anterior to the appearance of man on the earth, it is not easy to maintain that death was not, before the fall, the law of the animal world, as it has been ever since. One can scarcely assert that carnivora became carnivorous, and were distinguished from herbivora only after the fall of the first man, or ignore what the open bowels of the earth show us so plainly, namely, that the struggle for life has been the law of living beings ever since life appeared here below. It has been said that all these discoveries are the ruin of religion and of Christian faith. We do not think so. What disappears is the remains of an ancient philosophy, whilst these discoveries compel us, unless we separate ourselves entirely from the current thought of the century, to modify the theological formulas by means of which the Church has hitherto explained the origin and evolution of the universe.

There is, finally, a third intellectual revolution, that which is due to the modern historical method. If astronomy and geology have changed the perspective of the world in our eyes, modern criticism and exegesis have to the same extent upset that of the history of humanity, and pushed its origins farther into the background.

Bossuet's *Discourse on Universal History* remains an admirable book; but how narrow and incomplete does this so-called universal history seem to us to-day! What authority can be attributed to the chronology and the great framework of epochs in which it is set? How far has the origin of man been set back simply through the discoveries which have shown us the long and humble existence of pre-historic humanity! What relation can we conceive between Adam or Noah, on the one side, with their precise and short gene-alogies, and the cave-dwellers on the other? And what a new light has been thrown on human origins by the wonderful deciphering of the mysteries of ancient Egypt, by the revelations which have come to us from Assyria, and by the still more astonishing resurrection of the great Aryan family! As to the Bible, is it possible to ignore the essentially new light in which we see it since modern criticism has produced those wonderful works, either on the authorship and the date of the writings of the Old Testament, or on the origin of those of the New? We leave aside the smaller results, which may always lawfully be contested; we speak only of the general view, of the general idea which we all, without exception, are brought gradually to form of the religious inspiration of these books, taken separately, and of the canon in which they are bound up. Can we truly remain satisfied with the ancient apologetics which establish the divine authority of these writings by proving their literary authenticity? Must we not, on the contrary, profoundly modify our dogma of the biblical canon and that of inspiration, just as we have modified the dogma of creation?

But we must go yet further. The general application of the historical method has still wider and deeper consequences; it puts the questions which we have to discuss in a totally different light. Formerly people dealt with ideas—metaphysical ideas especially—as fixed and immutable quantities. With two notions and a few abstract theorems Descartes and Spinoza formed their conception of the world. To-day, our ideas, even the highest, no longer come before us with this absolute character; they are the result of a mental evolution that we can follow up in history. The human mind itself undergoes modification. Our ideas are only phenomena which must be explained by anterior phenomena. In other words, the notion of evolution in matters of philosophy has triumphed by means of the historical method; and to affirm the value of this notion applied to dogmas is the very object of this essay. To stand up against this historical law, which is the law of life, would be vain; we could not prevent it from asserting itself as a supreme power. Those who cling to dogmatic immutability are in the same position as the Roman cardinals who anathematised Galileo, and protested energetically against the movement of rotation of the earth. Neither these protestations nor the anathemas prevented the earth from turning, and the cardinals from turning with it. Such a blind resistance would be a great inconsistency for us as Protestants. The revision of dogmas, in principle as well as in fact, is still possible in the Churches founded by the Reformation; in principle, because in them the confessions of faith are all relative and remain subordinate to the Word of God; in fact, because the spirit of research, of criticism, and of free discussion has never ceased to breathe in Protestant theology, and breathes to-day more strongly than ever. This work of revision, then, will be accomplished; of this I have the fullest assurance. We may lack faith and courage to undertake it; but if we fail, God will raise up other workers. Christianity cannot perish; it has never failed to adapt itself to the state of mind and thought of past centuries; and it will find and create the dogmatic form which will suit future times.

It still remains for us to state what

share ought to be taken in this evolution of dogma by the teaching of dogmatics as it exists in our theological colleges.

III

Would it be right for professors in their classes to take no part in these crises of the Christian mind, and not to interfere in this process of evolution? Would it be wise to let it develop itself by the chance of circumstances and under the weight of outward necessities? Who can deny that the duty of every Church which is determined to be faithful to its mission lies in the opposite direction? Is it not for such a Church a need, as well as a right, to nourish a great and constant theological activity in its bosom, to take and to keep the initiative of these transformations, in order that they may be made according to the logic of the Church's principle and in the direct line of its tradition? Woe to the Churches which should fail to do this noble work in reference to themselves and to the inheritance bequeathed to them by the past! They would, sooner or later, fall victims to the universal law which they would have ignored.

In fact, nothing is less to be feared than this in the Protestant Churches. It is for that purpose that they have all instituted faculties of theology, and in these faculties a special course of study which is designated precisely by this word *dogmatics*. I hold that to teach dogmatics is to fill an ecclesiastical office. It is a ministry, a *charisma*[1] of the Church, one among many other ministries. The Church has possessed this

[1] Spiritual gift.

charisma from the beginning, and has never chosen to be without it. St. Paul, in enumerating the functions of the Church,[1] immediately after the functions of apostles and prophets, mentions that of *teachers.* This function of teaching dogmatics has been understood in different ways, and has taken different shapes according to the needs of the various times and countries. What it is important for us to understand is the place which it ought to occupy now, in order to comply with the necessities of our time. What is the task of dogmatics in the present day?

It must be owned that the teaching of dogmatics has grown infinitely in importance, in liberty, and, consequently, in responsibility. In the Middle Ages, when the

[1] 1 Cor. xii. 28.

teacher of dogma received his formulas from the infallible Church, or in the seventeenth century, when he drew them from the Bible, not only ready made but also divine and immutable, his task was simple enough. His whole ambition and effort consisted in arranging the dogmas in a logical order, so as to make them into a system and to accredit them as far as possible by means of reason and of syllogism. We may add that in the scholastic system he found a form perfectly adequate to his work. The scholastic system died together with the principle of an infallible external authority. The present task of Christian thinkers is altogether different. It consists chiefly in applying criticism to the old dogmas; in disengaging their vital principle; in preparing for this principle a new expression;

and, consequently, in taking the lead or lending its aid to this movement of dogmatic evolution of which we have just been speaking. And observe that this is no assertion of a disputed right, nor a self-imposed duty. The Church itself points out the way to the teacher of dogmatics; this is the service which it requires and expects from him. To-day, this criticism of dogmas constitutes in reality the main part of dogmatic teaching in all the Protestant Churches. It is worked out more or less successfully and conscientiously by one or another; but there is not a chair of dogmatics in which the inheritance of the past is received otherwise than as a legacy on which this debt of criticism is charged.

It is important to understand the nature and the object of this criticism of dogmas.

Its object is not to destroy dogmas, but to set free their living principle from the decaying form in which it is enclosed, and to prepare for it new forms in harmony with modern culture. Criticism does not formulate new dogmas—that is the business and the right of the Church; but it tries to render easy and free from danger the passage, which is always critical, between old and new ideas. And nothing seems more necessary at the moment through which we are passing. The forms of dogma begin to grow old from the day they are consecrated by general consent. As soon as a few years have passed, they need a translation and a commentary. By the fact that the Church lives on and continues her experiences through the ages, while the dogmatic formula, from the day when it is adopted, remains stationary, a sort of rupture, a disagreement more or less open, is produced almost immediately between this stationary formula and the conscience of the advancing Church. Who is to restore the equilibrium and create harmony? Who is to settle the terms of conciliation and make the transition between yesterday and to-day? Who is to knit together the chair which links the generations and the centuries, and to keep the dogma supple and malleable by bathing it constantly in the warmth of Church life? Who is to make peace in the communities and in the minds of the people by enlightening them? Must not this be done by the teaching of dogmatics so far as this teaching answers to its ideal?

To produce these satisfactory results, two conditions are equally necessary. The theologian must, on the one hand, be in communion with the scientific thought of his time. General culture, an open mind, a cordial feeling for the working out of human civilisation, are indispensable. But, on the other hand, it is just as essential that he should be in close communion with the life of his Church and have in himself the principle of that life. Since it is in his own soul that the religious principle of the Church and the philosophical thought of the time must meet and be united, he must belong, in a very real manner, to his time and to his Church. More specially he must live the life of the Church, because the dogmatic transformation in which he is collaborating cannot be accomplished from without and by a foreign or hostile power. It is tradition itself which must be developed in and by his teaching. The only way to criticise dogma positively is to do it not by reference to an external and profane standard, but by reference to the religious principle of the dogma and in the interest of that principle itself. That is to say that, according to my view, as soon as the theologian no longer grasps this principle in his mind and feels it in his heart, he is no longer qualified for the post of teacher of dogmatics.

I hope, then, my dear pupils (for it is to you that I would address these last words), that, in following these lectures on reformed dogmatics, you will constantly recognise, amidst many imperfections and failings, the fundamental principle and tradition of the piety of the Reformed Church. Yet it is possible that, notwithstanding our goodwill and our efforts, the criticism of dogma which we shall have to go through together, may bring some trouble and disquietude into your minds and consciences. Our religious education has been so conducted that our moral life may seem to be indissolubly knit up with such and such a dogmatic conception, the ruin of which may seem to be fatal to it. You must, in this case, firmly resist a precipitate judgment, which would be nothing but the result of illusion. It is not in our day only that ideas have had to be renewed, or that the Christian life has had to go on its way leaving behind it its antiquated forms. Let me conclude by repeating to you the story of the monk Serapion, which one of the Fathers of the Church has preserved to us, and which was recently recalled to our minds by M. Lobstein, our young and eminent colleague at Strasburg.

"The monk Serapion, a man full of zeal and piety, one day heard from the priest Paphnutius and the deacon Photinus that God, in the image of whom man had been created, was a Being without material body, or outward form, or organs of sense. The pious Serapion having declared himself convinced by the influence of catholic tradition and the force of the arguments developed before him, all those present rose up to give thanks to God for having saved such a holy man from the awful heresy of anthropomorphism. But as they were praying, the unfortunate old man, feeling the image of the God to whom he had been accustomed to address his prayers vanishing from his heart, was deeply troubled in spirit. He sobbed violently and fell to the ground, exclaiming in tears: 'Woe to me, unfortunate man! They have taken away my God, and now I have no one whom I can grasp, and I do not know whom I am to adore and pray to! *Heu me miserum! tulerunt a me Deum meum, et quem nunc teneam non habeo, et quem adorem aut interpellem.*'"

How deep and significant is this old story! What a striking symbol it is of our own experience and of the experience of humanity! It may be that we are all, though on various steps of the spiritual ladder, nothing more than idolaters like the good and pious Serapion. We always adore some sort of idol. If science comes and tears it away from us and destroys it, we stand perplexed and miserable, as if it had taken everything away from us. Let us be more manly. Are we not here to learn by experience that our religious life is independent of every image and theory, and that its source and end is the God who, while revealing Himself to our hearts, yet remains infinitely superior to all the conceptions of our mind? The everlasting complaint of piety disturbed in its habits or disappointed in its hopes is a cry like that of Mary Magdalene: "They have taken away my Lord, and I know not where they have laid Him." If these words occasionally come to our lips, and if this trouble agitates our hearts, let us remember that Christ is risen: His spirit, which is always living, is no longer dependent on a material and perishable frame. Let us repeat to ourselves that no truth in a special sphere can go counter to the truth itself, and let us walk faithfully forward, remembering that we are the disciples and the witnesses of Him who said: "God is a Spirit: and they that worship Him must worship in spirit and truth."

www.ingramcontent.com/pod-product-compliance
Lightning Source LLC
La Vergne TN
LVHW020653100826
845148LV00012B/2462

* 9 7 9 8 3 8 5 2 6 5 0 0 8 *